PRAISE ABOUT THE AUT...

"*Carolyn Thompson is a woman on a mission. She has a positive impact on everyone she meets. Carolyn's story of spiritual strength and hope will inspire you to push through when the unexpected happens.*"

Darren Hardy
Founding publisher/editor of SUCCESS *Magazine,* New York Times Bestselling Author, and Mentor to CEOs and High Achievers

"*I have often commented that if you are a family who farms or ranches and you care deeply about your family and your family operation, you really need to spend some time with Carolyn Thompson. She is truly the best I have ever seen at understanding the challenges that our farm and ranch families face and very importantly explaining the various options available to deal with those challenges. In addition to her outstanding professionalism, Carolyn is a woman of faith. As I, like so many others, shared her very difficult journey, I personally grew closer to God. Carolyn taught us the true meaning of courage, determination and faith. I can never thank her enough for her willingness to share. She is a very special person, who I am proud to call my friend.*"

Jim Woster
Influential Agriculture Writer, Broadcaster, Speaker

"Carolyn is one of the most passionate, focused, empathetic, professional women and mothers that I know. Despite numerous obstacles in life, she never saw anything but hope, dreams, and love of God. That translated directly into her support for my family's estate planning. Clear, concise, complete, and all with her heart and mind keeping our goals, our family, and our future in mind. Love of God, love of family, and a deep commitment to everyone she encounters, makes her a beacon of hope for us all. Thanks so much, Carolyn."

Dr. Dave Kapaska
Regional President & CEO of Avera McKennan

"Working with Carolyn has given us the confidence to know that we have provided adequately for our children while maximizing our philanthropic goals. She listens well, asks the right questions and has helped us create plans that fit with our personal mission: to be good stewards of all God has blessed us with for the benefit of the Kingdom. With that understanding and her technical knowledge, she has created estate plans unique to us and helped us modify them as goals evolve and life changes. Now that our children are older, we have family meetings to reaffirm our goals and the legacy plan we have in place."

Rob and Miriam Broin
Chairman and Chief Technology Officer at Otoka Energy

CUTTING

TO THE

CORE

CAROLYN THOMPSON

CUTTING

TO THE

CORE

FINDING WHAT MATTERS MOST
Through the Eyes of a Survivor
in Life & Business

THRONE
PUBLISHING GROUP

Throne Publishing Group
2329 N Career Ave #215
Sioux Falls, SD 57107
ThronePG.com

DEDICATION

To my three children, Taylor, Rachel and Will. You have brought more to my life and given me more purpose than you will ever know.
Love you always and forever, no matter what,
Mom

And to Seth, the unknown hero who gave me new life. There is no thank you big enough that I can give you, other than to do the best I can with this life and remember to rejoice always. May you feel God's blessings daily.

TABLE OF CONTENTS

INTRODUCTION

L et me begin by asking you a question: What would happen if you were plucked from your life this very moment? How would your family feel? How would your business fare? How would you handle leaving everything behind? I ask because it's a question I had to answer in reality, and it rocked my world.

In my work as an estate planning attorney, I've helped thousands of clients with estate and succession planning. We've carefully crafted plans to keep their families together and united, and their legacy well tended into the future. In all of my preparation for others, I never imagined at age 45 I'd be living out the planning I had done for myself.

However, by walking with God through harrowing times, I've gained so much more than I otherwise could have. By being challenged and led through difficult seasons, I've seen God's hand at work before my eyes. In this book, I'd like to share with you some of these stories. From starting my law practice to weathering the fiercest storm of my life, God has been at center stage. And He's often used the people I'm surrounded by to pour His love into me—so their stories have become part of mine, too.

My roots are in rural South Dakota, and I'm certainly a product of the prairie. As I'll share, I've had a lifelong love for farming communities like the one I'm from. In estate planning, I see hundreds of beautiful stories sit across the table from me each year. And my life's mission is to connect with them and help preserve the fruit of such incredible hard work.

I hope you both enjoy and benefit from the lessons I've learned. They certainly haven't been easy, but worthwhile things seldom are. I've discovered people must always take first place in life and business, and I invite you to see why I believe that's still true today.

PART ONE

FOUNDATION

1

COFFEE, FARMERS, AND SERVICE

So much of who we are can be traced to our roots. I'm from rural South Dakota, and no matter where I go, I bring those roots with me. I always say, "You can take the girl out of Parkston, but you can't take Parkston out of the girl." Growing up, I was just a regular kid in a small town, pouring coffee. This is still who I am, except now I practice law in four states. In my work in estate planning, my role isn't in dollars, trusts, and legalese. Instead, it's in family stories, legacies, and the stuff lives are made of. I help arrange futures where the story continues, passing to children and grandchildren. Beyond the paperwork are the people we serve, and first and foremost their legacy matters.

This book is a collection of stories that may look a lot like yours, with tales of hard work, victories, and defeats, and of building a business brick by brick, pouring my heart and soul into something lasting that I believed in. My journey has had some serious curves in the road—most of them unexpected. But it's in the curves that we find out who we really are and what we're made of. More importantly, we find out what we are made for. These words are dedicated to Thompson Law's story and the people who have helped make it what it is today. But what I've discovered is that it's simply a parallel to my own journey in life, discovering more of who I am and of who has helped shape me along the way.

I'll share testimonies of faith, God's love, and His guidance. I'll also pull back the curtain on some of the most trying times of my life. I have learned that when we have the courage to be vulnerable, we can truly connect and grow. My story started in small-town South Dakota and has continued to grow roots there. My practice of love and law will continue to grow because He wouldn't have it any other way.

CAFFEINATED ROOTS

I'd always had an industrious spirit, working as many jobs as there were hours in the day. As a child, my first career was in agriculture: selling my grandma's vegetables from her legendary garden to the neighborhood. She had a greenhouse that I worked at as well as three gardens in her backyard. After watering, weeding, and other work, I was allowed to sell some of the harvest on Fridays during the summers. With the money I earned from my gardening empire, and other jobs babysitting and my morning paper routes, I opened my first checking account. This was surprising, since I wasn't even

12 yet. However, I felt I'd officially joined the rank-and-file of work-ers. Life was good in Parkston.

With summer ending and a need to keep my checking account in the black, I asked my Aunt Carmen for a job at the Corner Cafe, which she and my Uncle Don owned at the time. To us, this wasn't any small-town diner, though. It was central to our family. From my grandma to an uncle to my folks, then to Uncle Don and Aunt Carmen, it seemed someone in our family had always owned the Corner Cafe. The heavy glass door swung open and shut, giving way to a bustling diner. Farmers and their families filtered in and out from morning till night each day, occupying classic vinyl booths and swivel chairs at the counter. The smell of Swiss steak and mashed potatoes over the noon hour was unmistakable. My job was to keep the four pots of coffee ever flowing, as I slipped in and out of the same conversations our patrons had each day. I also waited tables, getting the opportunity to exercise a memory that surprises me to this day. Because I didn't want the customers to see my poor hand-writing on the ticket, I filed orders away in my head and was able to perfectly recall them for parties of 10. Apart from coffee and service was also the occasional short straw I drew, though. I would have to scamper down the creaky, uneven steps into our basement to gather certain supplies—a musty dungeon with draw-string lights, gravel floor, and enough shadows for a girl's imagination to run amok. But it was all part of the job.

Routine settled in Parkston, like in many other small towns. The same faces made regular appearances, some stoic and quiet, others animated and chatty. And the Corner Cafe played host to our friends, family, and farmers each day. I do remember one change that ruffled some feathers and upset the coffee cart, however.

For the longest time, the cafe's coffee was bottomless. So we'd serve cup after cup while the patrons talked about the weather or the coming harvest. But when I was 12 or so, we raised the price per cup from 15 cents to a whopping 25 cents—and on top of that, instituted a two-refill policy. Now, from the outside, this might not sound like much. But as a 12-year-old girl, breaking this news to burly farmers that they'd have to pay another quarter to keep drinking coffee wasn't fun.

JUGGLING DONUTS IN THE SNOW

I kept the job at the cafe into high school but squeezed in others along the way. Money was always tight in my family, so if I wanted to drive or pay for gas, car repairs, car insurance, or wear the clothes I liked, I had to forge my own path. But this never bothered me; it was simply how my life worked. From extra paper routes to landing the coveted job at Statz Drug that only picked up one new high school employee every other year, long days were routine. The longest, though, was the stretch where I worked Saturdays at "JR's Rec Center" in the early morning, then the lunch rush at the cafe, followed by my shift at Statz and then back to JR's Rec for the evening. These sixteen-hour days kept me hopping, but I was glad for the hours and income.

One Saturday morning, I woke up well before 6:00 a.m. as usual, this time in the dead of winter. Parkston was buried beneath a blanket of snow thigh high, and I had a day of shifts ahead of me. Layered up in a snowmobile suit and boots, I trudged from our apartment on the edge of town down the highway. The highway was easy walking because it had been plowed, but block after block I looked for a plowed street to make my passage downtown easier. No such luck, so I trudged through six blocks of snow.

Finally, I made it to good ol' Main Street. I got the heaping tray of donuts from the bakery and walked them over to the rec center. Drenched in sweat, I peeled off the layers of clothes and started the coffee pots at the cafe.

This necessity-breeds-opportunity lifestyle instilled a South Dakota work ethic in me by default. It also made me independent, teaching me to rely on my own work, to budget income and expenses, and to discern needs from wants. There was no notion of waiting for a handout. This was further reinforced by my parents' somewhat surprise divorce. I knew this was an especially difficult time for my mom, because people in a town like ours simply didn't get divorced. It wasn't done. So when this happened, I could sense she felt, as I felt, branded by a big red "D" on her chest. My dad moved to nearby Mitchell, SD, so we wouldn't be too far from each other. However, what happened in the following years served to balance my self-sufficiency with an appreciation for the unexpected help I did receive.

SLIPPING THROUGH THE CRACKS

As my high school career drew to a close, I set my sights on college. I'd done well in school, and like many of my friends, was fully prepared to get all the student financial aid I needed. After all, my family wasn't wealthy, so I was confident that I'd qualify for the necessary grants and loans. Then came the devastating news of the double-edged sword my tenacity proved to be. I learned that I didn't qualify for all of the aid I needed because I was somehow *above* the income threshold. With my income they declared me "legally independent." I had worked so hard to support myself that I had personally risen above the threshold. I was a waitress and a clerk, not a child actor for goodness' sake; but the limits were the limits.

I didn't give up without a fight, however. I called, petitioned, and sent letters to all of the powers-that-be who my grandma, my school counselor, and I could think of. But I heard the same news over and over: "We're so sorry for your situation. Unfortunately, there's nothing we can do. It seems like you've slipped through the cracks." I was so sick of hearing that phrase, "You've slipped through the cracks," but it played on repeat. After I'd exhausted all of my remedies, I was still $2,000 short of my tuition. I still remember that sinking feeling that all I'd planned was falling through. Then, at the eleventh hour, my grandma came swooping in and gave me the money to cover my shortfall. I'm still so grateful to her. She, along with my folks, taught and modeled a work-hard-and-never-give-up attitude.

A THOUSAND BEAUTIFUL STORIES

I went to school at Northern University and studied Business Management and Accounting. There I learned about the estate tax system. All I could think about was the many farming families I knew who worked so hard, and went through so much, only to get the big left hook of estate taxes when they die. I knew few people put together wills, trusts, or estate plans. Living in small town anywhere, it is so easy for people to put that off. This realization spurred me to commit to law school and work in this field. I worked just as hard in my undergraduate studies, and it paid off in a big way, earning me a full-ride scholarship to law school at the University of South Dakota. As I pored through thousands of pages and sat through the stream of classes, I saw an opportunity to help.

After graduating, I focused on what's now become my core identity: I just want to keep a family a family—guard them as best I can from those surprise left hooks—and help them face the reality of their life and their planning needs. My area of practice provides me a unique vantage and ability to help. We deal with real people who have real lives and our goal is to make a real difference for them. One of my appointments in years past is a shining example of this.

One day a big, strapping farmer with a cowboy hat just as big sat across the table from me. We reviewed some of his particulars together and I learned that he'd accomplished an incredible amount in his lifetime. However, within one hour this hulking man was sobbing in my office. He relayed to me that when he was in college, his father passed away. This forced him to quit and return home to rebuild the farm. He sacrificed another career trajectory entirely to keep his family's legacy alive. But then his younger brother somehow convinced their mother to gift, sell, and leave his younger brother all the family land. Literally all. This cut him and the other siblings out entirely, fracturing their relationship. But being the resilient work-horse that he was, he began anew and built a second operation. His tears, though, were a plea for an estate plan that prevented the same wounds from being inflicted among his family and five children.

Cloaked in the duty of confidentiality, this scene has replayed itself from every year of practice onward. The wounds of past gen-erations don't evaporate on their own, and at Thompson Law we unearth them and deal with them together. When clients allow me to cut, gently, to the core, I can design a plan authentic to them, helping them build the legacy they want to leave. Just like in my grandma's garden, sometimes we have to do some weeding before we can get to harvest. My role has always been to have technical mas-tery in my practice but to let that be the unseen foundation for the plan we build together. And because I'm real and vulnerable about my own wounds, they can be too. Together, we work within a safe environment.

I'm not interested in legalese or creating a Downton Abbey-like façade. Instead, I remember that we're all beautiful, broken children fully loved by God. Beyond the paper are the people, and people are what matter. Together, we build something that shares, designs, builds, and protects hard-earned legacies. This means that our DNA at Thompson Law has become something that doesn't see volumes of clients or billable hours as our metrics for success. Instead, every person who walks through our doors is a new book, a fresh story. People are so much more than a balance sheet. I see beautiful life stories to be honored and guarded, and I love being a part of it. We are helping to complete one of the final chapters in

their book, and the plan must honor them and position their ben-
eficiaries well.

Because numbers and succession plans represent lives poured out
in service, hard work, and fortitude, it is important that we design an
estate plan that honors the whole person. When clients share their
journey with us—where they're from and where they want to go—
we can craft values statements and ethical wills rather than plans
that divide, dump, and destroy. When we really connect with them,
it is just like serving that hot coffee, alongside the gooey, Sunday-
special caramel rolls. In so many ways I'm still that girl keeping the
donut tray filled and the coffee flowing. It doesn't matter if I am at
a national convention on estate planning or entrepreneurship, or in
my Sioux Falls, SD, office, my people are still my people. I just serve
them in different ways.

2 LOVE AND LAW

My professional roots are intertwined with South Dakota soil as well. Out of law school, I landed a wonderful position at the oldest practicing law firm in the state. There, I carved out a niche for myself practicing in estate planning. Life seemed good on the outside. My career was going well. I liked my partners—and had become the firm's youngest one. Soon, I found myself at 32 years old with two children and another baby on the way, debating whether I was really at the right place in my life.

THE LORD LED THE WAY

I knew staying in a traditional practice would mean giving up being the mom I wanted to be, and that was a trade I could not make. If I was going to be the lawyer, business owner, mother, and wife that

I wanted to be, something needed to change. So my due diligence began. I feverishly wrote pros and cons lists, consulted with friends, and listened to trusted advisors. What became abundantly clear was that I was really not a lawyer, per se. I was an entrepreneur with the heart of a teacher who happened to practice law. However, to leave and start a practice of my own was no small feat.

I continued with market research, strategizing, dreaming, and making lists, but the aha moment occurred when my first child, Taylor, then age four, walked up to me with a Bible I'd never seen before. I opened it and found a note on the inside cover that a teacher had written. It read, "Trust in the LORD with all your heart and lean not on your own understanding; in all your ways acknowledge Him, and He will make your paths straight" (Prov. 3:5). And there it was. I threw away the lists, thanked my friends and counselors, and felt completely at peace about where the Lord was leading me. On December 31, 2002, I left the firm with their blessing and goodwill and knew I was stepping squarely into a new adventure with God. I gave up earthly security for the greater security that's only found in following His lead. But just like that early morning trudge through thigh-high snow in Parkston, and the sixteen-hour climbs to college, building Thompson Law has been anything but easy. But things built to last never are.

SO IT BEGINS

Thompson Law, P.C. officially opened its doors in a leased space on January 1, 2003, with just one employee and myself. But here's the thing; as in most businesses, the busy seasons ebb and flow, and January generally brings more ebb than flow! However, I was a woman on a mission, and we were on the clock. At eight months pregnant, I had to bring in some revenue to spend the six weeks maternity time I wanted with my five-year-old son Taylor, sixteen-month daughter Rachel, and soon-to-be baby number three in February.

In that first month, though, I realized that more important than metrics was focusing on the clients, taking care of them, and trusting God to provide. When my brand changed, it became evident that we were going to grow fast. People knew they were dealing with me, and as my team grew, they could rely on the same treatment and care. This was critical to our growth and still is today. I founded the business on the core values of faith, family and firm. Any decisions we made must filter through and honor them.

I created a firm solely dedicated to estate planning and business succession. We were the first "boutique" estate planning law firm in the state. Our goal was simple: keep a family a family. From here, I developed a passion for agricultural estate planning—well before it was popular and well before corn prices skyrocketed, causing the land prices to do the same.

See, I always knew that, whether land was $500 or $5,000 an acre, land was land, and God only made so much of it. If a family wanted to keep themselves and their farming operations viable, we needed to put pencil to paper and design new ways of managing farm estates. While there was once a day where a farming son who had 25 percent equity in the land could go to the bank and finance the buyout of his siblings, that day was gone. I didn't want the families I served to fall into the "nothing will" that simply read, "in equal shares to my children." This resonated with people, and we gained traction.

Over the next few years, we scaled up quickly, and I knew I was achieving where I wanted to be as a mother and a lawyer, but maybe a bit sleep deprived. And I was starting to live in that space of fulfillment. So it didn't make sense to me to pay rent into the indefinite future—especially a 40-plus-year future. So I began to pray about a solution, and the idea of buying land and constructing a building of our own took shape. After finding a nearby commercial lot in a wonderful location, I explored the idea further. I was so busy with our firm, though, that the appointment took weeks to schedule. But finally, the listing agent, Raquel Blount with Lloyd Companies, and I had a date set to walk the property. Something odd happened then.

Even though I'd waited for weeks to see this property, on the Friday before our Tuesday appointment I felt a nudge from the Lord that I needed to see it sooner. By this time, I knew enough to trust Him, even in these seemingly small details. So I called the agent and she, like me, was absolutely booked solid except for one sliver of time after church on Sunday. And there we found ourselves picking our way across the dirt, talking details, both of our families in tow. She was tremendously accommodating. Afterward, I was satisfied with my choice and felt good about moving slowly ahead—*then Monday came.*

BUILDING WITH STEEL AND STONE

It was a hectic day, filled with appointments and running a growing business, and my agent came in with urgent news. "Another offer came in on the land, Carolyn," she said, "so if you want it you're going to have to put in an offer now." My head spun but I knew we had to move on it. See, God knew I had to see it before Tuesday. So we put in an offer and got the deal. But now, I had to figure out how to finance both the land and the building, so I was pushing off closing for as long as I could.

We were successful in what we set out to do for people and the practice, and its permanence was taking shape. However, the coming spring and summer would be two of the most difficult seasons of my life.

While things were grand in my practice, life at home had become increasingly tough. I didn't want to wear the scarlet letter "D" (divorce), which led me to stay in a failing marriage for far too long. And what had been a difficult marriage now led to an extremely difficult divorce. But I learned a lot and have found peace on the other side. I clung to the truth that healing and growth always comes—and it did for me. However, while this was happening I was trying to secure financing at the same time as meeting with architects, finding tenants, raising my children—oh, and still running my business. But in His kindness, the Lord spoke to my heart, challenged me, and didn't let me take the easy way out—which would have been leaving the building project on the table. Even though I wanted to give it up at times, He pressed me to fight on.

Craig Lloyd, a developer, was instrumental in helping me as the plans came together. I made so many big decisions. I was committed to a quality structure built of steel, concrete, and brick rather than wood. However, this came with a price tag that was hundreds of thousands of dollars costlier. Though a wooden building would have alleviated significant financial burdens on the front end, it would end up in a structure with a short shelf life. This wasn't how I wanted to operate. After all, when skimping on quality, people usually pay twice.

Another difficulty arose when I learned that the total square footage of a building is limited by the amount of parking provided. We needed a parking space for each 300 square feet inside the building, which meant we would have to have underground parking, another $250,000 hurdle, for this place to even remotely cash flow. The project was overwhelming and the divorce proceedings were unending. I couldn't do this building, but He could.

At a spiritual retreat, I met with a lay minister, and she listened as I talked through the situation. I knew the Lord was calling me to move forward with the building. Then she asked one of those simple, but profoundly insightful, questions that are unforgettable. She asked, "Carolyn, are you afraid to commit to a building or to commit to God?" And there it was! I immediately released it to God and let Him keep writing the story.

This certainly didn't mean I had it easy. If you've ever applied for a commercial loan of any size, you can sympathize with my situation. The few assets I had were frozen due to the divorce, which left me with a shortfall on the down payment—*oddly reminiscent of my struggle to get student loans*. But I left no stone unturned. I took out credit cards with 0 percent interest and maxed them out, got court approval to max out on a home equity line of credit, and made the numbers work as best as I could. On the heels of this decision two things happened. The Lord brought to me and we worked with what are, to this day, the two biggest cases of my life; that meant the revenue was there. And second, our contractor, Pete Hoogendoorn, miraculously found place after place where we could shave tens of thousands of dollars from the bill without sacrificing quality. I had to step out for God to step in. This was His building. Then, we broke ground and moved in April of 2006.

CLARITY

I learned so much through this process. The details that needed to come together were staggering, and to weigh them while running a business and managing a complicated life was difficult. But I believe that the more we allow God to stretch and grow us, the more He gives—and He can manifest in the most amazing people. Through this and so many other harrowing stories, I've learned that there are so many biblical principles that apply to both law and entrepreneurship. After all, "to whom much [is] given . . . much will be required" (Luke 14:48).

Today, from the first step into Thompson Law, that belief is clearly reflected. Among the warm, family-room-style reception area and coffee bar furnishings lies an open Bible with a yellow highlighter next to it. One of our favorite things is when people go to mark their favorite passage of Scripture, and then thumb through the pages to see the golden words already chosen by others. It's so encouraging to see this book dappled with color from hundreds of hands, hands that have held their own Bibles as they've made decisions on how to live and who to trust.

First and foremost, I believe that God has a calling for each of us, and our part is simply to trust Him and obey. At so many points, His promise and still, small voice was all I had to cling to. But cling I did. Now I see that period of Thompson Law, and my life, with crystal clarity. God has always been four steps ahead of me.

Faith is not saying, "Father, lay it all out and then I will go." Faith is saying, "Father, I don't see a way, but I trust you and if you say go, I will go." I am in the trust business, but my ultimate trust is in Him. When God leads, it is a wonderful dance between what He's done and what we do. When I spend time with my clients, initially there is confusion, struggle, and challenge at the tough decisions that need to be made. However, I revere the chances I get to help a family build an estate or business succession plan that honors them and their legacy. Their trust in me is not taken lightly. When we make the extra effort to touch every area of their lives that's important to them, I know we're fulfilling God's purpose for that building of steel and stone. I trust we're laying the foundation for legacies built to last.

In the years that followed our building's completion, the Lord blessed us with tremendous growth. And after nine short years, the beginning of 2015 saw us at the pinnacle of our firm. Little did we know that on the eve of our biggest event, we were on the cusp of another trial-filled season, one that would test us to see what we were really made of. Were we built of steel and stone, too, or frames of wood? As the psalmist wrote millennia ago, "Unless the LORD builds the house, the builders labor in vain" (Psalm 127:1a).

3 | WHEN WE DON'T KNOW WHY

The Lord helped us build both a building and a practice made to last. His faithfulness was so obvious, and His leading so clear, my faith increased tenfold. Little did I know I'd have even more opportunity to grow. When we face trials and hardships, we're offered opportunities to deepen, to expand our roots and become more than we were before. But it's not comfortable and almost always unexpected. Rarely is tragedy scheduled on the calendar. It was time for another twist in my story—or should we say growth opportunity?

We had successfully navigated the monumental building project and its attendant obstacles. The space we had created became a true home to our core mission. In the time that followed, our firm steadily grew. We carved out a unique footprint in succession planning before it became mainstream to do so, and our outlook was bright. Thompson Law had nowhere to go but up, and all signs were trending that way.

THE BEGINNING

In the spring of 2015, business was booming. Every day, I had the chance to meet with new families and help them approach their estate succession and legacy in empowering ways. We were seeing strong families become even stronger and fences being mended that were long overdue for maintenance. This has always been the focal point of my work and my favorite part. Being able to help families stay families was both exciting and fulfilling. And we were doing so with more clients than ever.

The firm was growing by the day, and we were at the pinnacle of our work to date. In fact, I was retaining ten out of ten clients on a regular basis (which is a bit unheard of). The Lord was blessing us and the families we served tremendously. Personally, things were flourishing as well. I'd been invited into an entrepreneurial group called the High Performance Forum. It was created, developed, and led by the world-renowned Darren Hardy, former publisher of *SUCCESS* magazine and business luminary.

I still communicate with my entrepreneur friends to this day, but it's always wowed me that I have such amazing associations. This was especially true when Darren handpicked only 24 people to an elite group. I joined multi-billionaires, executives of Fortune 500 companies, and leaders at the forefront of their field. I was beyond honored.

We met regularly, and I gained more value than I'd thought possible. This was another loop on the thread of amazing people God's placed in my life. However, one event in particular stood apart from the rest.

All of us met in Florida and began the event playing golf at Trump International. Not only is this one of the premier courses in the world—I played the best round of my life! I was out-driving the guys and having an incredible time beneath the Florida sun. After this amazing day, though, the evening turned for me.

When I returned to my hotel, I started feeling sick. As the night progressed, I felt more sick than I'd ever felt in my life. My stomach twisted in excruciating pain. I rested on day two of our conference but was still feeling so terrible I thought of missing the evening dinner and sessions. It was held at Donald Trump's Mar-a-Lago mansion, and our speaker was John Maxwell. A few colleagues encouraged me not to miss spending time at such an amazing place and talking with these world-class entrepreneurs.

The dinner was impeccable, with courses of beautiful seafood and one-of-a-kind dishes paired with perfect wines—and all prepared by a world-class chef. However, I had become so ill, I could only stomach a bit of broth the chef was kind enough to prepare. I pushed through, thinking it was just an unfortunate case of the flu. In my mind, it was a small hang-up inconsequential to my life.

The sickness persisted into the next day, though, and I decided to call my doctor in South Dakota for some insight. I didn't want this to inhibit the rest of our sessions and time together. After we spoke, he counseled me to visit a clinic, have a few labs run and the results sent to him. I did so and didn't think anything more of it.

THE BIOPSY

Upon returning to South Dakota, my doctor called and asked that I have a few more labs done. I was feeling better but weak. My stomach issues had subsided, and I did lab work on a Wednesday. These labs then led to more lab tests that Thursday. These visits were happening pretty fast. I had been working on a life insurance policy to give to charity before my Florida trip, and it just so happened I signed the policy in between these doctor visits.

At this point, I was still unconcerned about my illness and saw it more as an annoyance. This was because I'd been given a preferred-plus health rating for my insurance policy. This category is associated with excellent health. In fact, some companies call it elite preferred or super preferred. I was strong, in great physical condition, and had no chronic problems. Nonetheless, I arrived at the doctor's office that Thursday for my next round of tests.

My results still troubled my doctor. My symptoms suggested anemia, but the numbers weren't adding up. After this appointment, the doctor expressed that he'd like to do a bone marrow biopsy. This was a surprise, and right after he said it, a little voice whispered, "Ask if you can do it today. . . ." So I followed the prompt. And by a scheduling miracle, I was able to get right in—which I was told *never* happens. I went, had the biopsy, and hit the ground running.

See, all this time that I was working in Florida, running my practice in Sioux Falls, and flitting from doctor to doctor, my team and I were preparing for a huge summit we were hosting. We had over 500 clients who would be attending; not only that, but the event was happening the next day, the Friday immediately after my biopsy.

In the flurry, we were preparing content for sessions, and I was writing my keynote. Our firm was poised for even more growth, and just as exciting, this was some of the best content I'd ever created in my life. I had a special sense that it would have a profound effect for many of my clients who would attend. My plan wasn't conveying simple information, but helping in transformation.

The event was called Reflect & Connect and was built upon the central theme of helping our clients share their legacy during their lives with those they loved—not simply planning on what would happen on paper after their passing. Our sessions were filled with digging deeper into family bonds, sharing gratitude, and making true connections that didn't exist before. But in the hustle of preparation for this enormous event, I received news that would rock my world.

THE NEWS THAT ROCKED MY WORLD

It's so easy to see with tunnel vision when defining career moments are on the horizon. I was sick but so focused on making the event valuable to all in attendance, I never stopped to consider that maybe my sickness wasn't anemia. So when my doctor called Thursday evening, concern filling his voice, I had to stop and listen.

I answered the phone, and the first words he said were, "This is going to rock your world. You have acute myeloid leukemia and it is six-to-eight-weeks terminal if left untreated. And Carolyn, if you didn't have this event tomorrow, I'd have you in the hospital tonight."

I sat stunned for a moment and wrote notes on my yellow legal pad as I had done for so many clients in the past—except this time it was me getting the call. My office was filled with my staff, busy prepping for our event. But all I could do was sit and ask myself, "Is this for real?" My doctor continued, describing the treatment plan.

He said, "Right after your event, you'll need to undergo 30 consecutive days of hospitalization in an isolation unit so you can undergo intense chemotherapy. Your immune system will be very weak, and you can't afford to have any germs in your environment."

I finished our brief conversation and pulled my thoughts together. I made the instant decision that I wouldn't tell my kids until after the event, but I opened up to a few of my staff. I knew this was serious, but I didn't fully accept the gravity of the situation until I saw the teardrops of some of my team members. This was a surreal moment.

Earlier in the week I was blessed with the chance to spend engaging time with some of the world's top business performers. I was privileged to gain access to their experience and even offer insight of my own. Thompson Law was experiencing a meteoric rise and quickly becoming a regional estate planning and legacy succession authority. Tomorrow, I had 500 clients coming to attend what would be a transformative event. Yet there I sat, surrounded by my team working shoulder to shoulder, with this blood cancer secretly flowing through every part of my body.

Not only this, but immediately after the event, I'd planned a dream sabbatical. I'd worked so hard, and now in the twentieth year of my law practice, I had a three-week respite with my children planned on the Island of Dominica. I had the house rented, plane tickets purchased—I was ready. We had an adventure-filled itinerary full of hiking, biking, whitewater rafting, and exploring. And afterwards, I was scheduled to hike the Grand Canyon rim to rim in support of a cancer fundraiser called Wacky Warriors; the irony wasn't lost on me.

I set my jaw, however, and pressed on.

REFLECT AND CONNECT

My doctor told me that during my keynote address, I couldn't walk out from behind the podium, nor could I leave the stage while other speakers presented. My strength was rapidly declining; I was freezing, needed a blood transfusion, and it was likely I would collapse if I didn't hold on to something firm for balance. I knew I wouldn't be the dynamic speaker I usually was, animated and moving back and forth across the stage. I just kept telling myself, "It is their day." I knew this event was going to make a lasting impact for them, even if I wasn't at the top of my game.

I still remember taking the stage and gripping the podium tightly. I looked across a sea of over 500 expectant faces and binders ready to be filled with notes. I saw their looks of reflection and knew they were deeply engaged—and on levels they never expected. Though I didn't move from behind the podium, I expressed my heart for them, and they responded beautifully. Hundreds of lives and families were strengthened despite my weakness.

I was able to be off the stage during lunch, and I rested on a makeshift air bed my team set up backstage. The day was incredible, and besides my need for extra rest, things went off without a hitch. It had been a monumental task to prepare for this in the midst of everything that happened. But still, my team came through in a major way and made that a landmark moment in the history of both my life and Thompson Law.

To cap the day off, we had a foreign exchange student named Lucy living with us, and she had prom that night. So we took pictures, smiled, laughed, and wished her well. Then it was time to rest and face the next season of my life. It certainly wasn't the sabbatical I'd planned. But I was determined to tackle it just as I did everything else.

BUILDING, NOT BREAKING

In reflection, the timing of this was stunning. The day before I got the worst health news of my life, I'd received a preferred-plus health rating. Today, I realize this could happen to anyone. I was plucked out of my life without a moment's notice. One day I was healthy, strong, and vibrant on paper. The next, I was given less than two months to live if I didn't undergo extreme chemotherapy, and there was no guarantee of survival.

The chapters in my life continually surprise me, but what I am learning is that God's faithfulness should be no surprise. I'd been through a great deal already to this point, and He'd seen me through.

From starting Thompson Law, to constructing our building of quality materials despite the odds, and to celebrating both the success of us and our clients, I'd lived a lot of life. Now, however, was another challenging chapter.

Instead of soaking in the sun with my children I was being pumped with poison and had very limited contact with the outside world. I've learned that everything can change in a blink, but I have been deepened because of this. My questions for those around me have become, "Are you ready to be plucked from your life right now? Have you invested in the things that truly matter?" The answers are so important because the stakes are so high. So what's your answer? Are you ready? Have you said what needs to be said?

PART TWO

A LEADER WHO
FOLLOWS

4

THE RADICAL
SABBATICAL

I nstead of the tropical vistas of Dominica, I found myself alone in a hospital room. I was hooked up to chemo 24 hours per day for seven days straight. Rather than the dense warmth of a Caribbean island, I was shivering in a sterile room with a metallic taste on my tongue. Yet I was grateful to be alive and to have caught the cancer before it progressed any further.

My restful sabbatical was swapped out for a more radical—and grueling—one. I also had a longer path ahead of me than I realized. During my first stint of chemo, I learned that it wasn't going to be 30 days of treatment only. Instead, that was just the first piece, and most people needed to step out of their lives for a minimum of nine to twelve months, if all went well. It was already hard enough to be away from my kids for a month, let alone for this unknown future. On top of this, I faced the ugly reality of the cancer treatment itself.

The goal of chemotherapy is to kill all cell production in its tracks. This is why hair falls out, because it's literally poisoning the entire body. People experience uncontrollable flailing, cold sweats, nausea, and many other unpleasant side effects I will leave unnamed. I gained 19 pounds of fluid in my first two days in treatment. Still, I did everything I was supposed to do, from constant water intake to sufficient protein ingestion, even though I felt ill. My mind was set; I wouldn't be the missing link in my regimen of care. Mentally, I prepared for a marathon, rather than a sprint. First things first, I needed to ensure my team was well equipped to run the race alongside me.

PREPARATIONS

True to myself, in the first week of treatment I sprinted ahead of my absence at the firm. Before the real wham-bam of chemo set in, I created guidelines for communication releases and developed a system of scheduling and note taking. I had to understand how I would function in this new normal. I had to pay attention to an entirely new set of performance metrics.

Rather than only numbers from inside the firm, I now watched my lab results, too—especially during chemo. Gone were the days where my calendar was filled with new clients, team meetings, and public speaking events. Now it was all about how my body would respond to the chemotherapy.

Throughout this time, my Thompson Law team was absolutely amazing. They understood my creative juices and knew if I was going to keep some semblance of my life, I'd have to keep them flowing. So from my hospital bed I created systems and strategies, and they were right there to help me make them into a reality. I drew ideas of what we needed, and they created them and sent them back to me. Then back and forth we went until the idea was polished and in working order. I was never one to lie still and do nothing. So if I couldn't go to the office, I brought the office to me. My sister Cheryl immediately stepped into my parental responsibilities, and she grew angel wings as she had to see her once-invincible sister ravaged by chemo and infections.

For your free copy of this tool, called "Joy of the Journey," visit www.cathompsonlaw.com/ joyofthejourney

THE LONG ROAD AHEAD

My team was invaluable to me throughout my treatment, especially in this first portion. My life was a whir of doctors, nurses, and beeping machines. A primary concern was avoiding infection. Even using the bathroom was a big production. I had to be assisted by a nurse, have machines rolled into place, and then escorted on a rickety walk across the cold tile floor. However, one night a nurse pulled back my blankets to help me use the restroom only to find blood everywhere. Because I was covered in so many blankets, I didn't feel the blood getting soaked up into them. Two of the lines in a catheter near my neck somehow opened, and this was bad—really bad. About every other day I was getting blood transfusions, and now I had lost a lot of blood in the night.

Fortunately, the nurse caught it, closed the lines, cleaned me up, and then helped me to the bathroom. Unfortunately, she didn't stay with me. In the process, I passed out from blood loss and hit my head. She found me unconscious on the hard, tile floor and apparently lifted me back into bed. I awoke surrounded by doctors and nurses with wide, concerned eyes. They told me that if I hadn't awoken when I did, I would not be eligible for my next, and most important, stage of treatment. I again reveled in God's timing to wake me just in time.

MY FINAL PLEA

I remember well the doctors' disappointment as the initial round of chemotherapy failed to stop the bad blasts (or cancer cell production in the bone marrow). Further testing found I had a rare gene translocation, with only 40 reported cases, making my treatment plan a bit of shooting in the dark. The next stage in my journey was secured by help from close friends in my entrepreneurial group. Thankfully, one of my colleagues had a close connection with two world-renowned doctors. With his help, my case was fast-tracked to the top leukemia cancer center in the world, MD Anderson Cancer Center in Houston, Texas.

My health was still touch and go, however, and as usual, time was of the essence. Now that the doors had opened to MD Anderson, I had to get there. I was told early on that most AML patients die from infection, not the cancer and, at this point, infections were raging in my body. However, my medical air transport was not going to be available for the journey from Sioux Falls to Houston for another four days. My local doctor replied, "She doesn't have four days." God miraculously intervened again, and a plane came available that night. I remember the case worker being in awe of how the doors were opening—and I simply said, "That's how my God works."

However, I was extremely weak and sick, and my good friend Mike Luken brought the kids to the hospital so I could say goodbye. Mike, like many, took every step of this journey with me. While I might have been alone—*I knew I wasn't really*. We had no idea what Houston would hold for us. Fighting through the exhaustion, I spent a little time with each of my children alone. It wouldn't be the last memory I wanted them to have of me—so I couldn't let it be.

The plane had to be meticulously cleaned because of my susceptibility to infection. On top of that, there was such a tight weight limit on this small plane that it only had space for two pilots, an EMT, myself, and one other passenger. My sister came with me, but I couldn't bring anyone or anything else. Incredibly, I couldn't even bring my Bible because it pushed us over the weight limit.

I recall being rolled into the fuselage in a coffin-like bed. I was strapped in tight and freezing down into my bones. It was a cold like I'd never experienced before. While being wheeled into the plane I heard a familiar voice yell, "I love you, CAT Woman—God's got this!" My dear friend Mary Howard waited and waited in the aviation parking lot for those few seconds to encourage me. My head swam with pain, and I felt cut off from everything. My kids and family, my business, and my friends—they all felt a million miles away.

I kept one thought at the center of my mind, though, and it was about my children: *I will survive for them.* Nothing was more important to me, and I'd simply accepted this as the next step of reaching my goal to coming home and growing with them. At that moment, I couldn't help but feel cheated, because when my kids were young I had to work so hard to keep my practice afloat and to struggle through a failing marriage. I'd done everything I could to sustain both, but at a price. So now, I couldn't let the opportunity to be with them slip away.

However, I did prepare for the worst. I was fortunate that my children had a deep understanding of God and His love. So I was confident that if I passed away, they wouldn't lose faith. Still, I recorded what would be my final plea to them should I die:

> You know I love you and that we love the Lord. But you cannot be angry. If the Lord says it's time for me to come home, you have to trust Him in that. But the most important thing is that you keep your faith in the Lord.

I arranged for a friend to give the voice recording to them if I didn't make it. But there was truly nothing else I wanted for my children other than for them to be rooted and grounded in the Lord. In the end, that was the only thing that mattered. If you have children, what would you tell them as your final words? As their mother, I knew these words had to be my sole hope for their lives. And they were. Money didn't matter; having meaning did.

In that moment, I remembered Jesus's words in Matthew 11:30 and felt peace: "... my yoke is easy, and my burden is light." Now more than ever, I needed Him to come through, and He did. I weathered the flight from the Great Plains to the Gulf Coast and went straight to the cancer center upon landing.

THROUGH THE FLAMES

The medical team immediately covered me with ice packs when I arrived at MD Anderson. Even though I was freezing cold, my body was burning a dangerously high fever. I can still remember the faces of the first doctors I saw, and they had fear in their eyes. From the moment of my arrival, however, I chose to reject that fear. I wasn't naïve and understood how tough this was going to be, but I needed to control my attitude from the outset. I repeated to myself over and over, "God is going to have a great and mighty purpose in this." And I believed it.

The initial stages of treatment at MDA were intense. It was a feverish blur of specialists with an all-hands-on-deck mentality. They didn't have a second to lose because they didn't know how many I had left. I spent 46 consecutive days in the hospital with an IV and much of it in excruciating pain. At the end of this time, the doctors pulled together in a roundtable to discuss next steps, but even with all of their experience, they didn't know what to do. Their decision was to throw the kitchen sink of treatment regimens at me. I was young, healthy, and muscular, so they deemed it my best option at beating this rare form of cancer.

If you've spent much time in hospitals, you've likely seen the whiteboards in every room. The nurses use them to write treatment plans and chart other pertinent information as a simple way to communicate. So the first time my nurse wrote the doctors' kitchen-sink treatment plan, she stopped in her tracks. She couldn't believe it was right and said, "This is wicked!"

That wasn't the most reassuring thing to hear. However, the Lord was right there. That day, I received first one message, and then another message from people with the same passage of Scripture laid on their hearts for me, Isaiah 43:1-2, which reads:

Fear not, for I have redeemed you;
I have called you by name, you are mine.
When you pass through the waters, I will be with you;
and through the rivers, they shall not overwhelm you;
when you walk through fire you shall not be burned,
and the flame shall not consume you.

That evening, I watched the live stream of Lucy's high school graduation ceremony, my exchange student's. And wouldn't you know it? That was their Scripture theme as well. I often ask the Lord to be loud, be clear and be repetitive. I don't want to miss His message . . . and there it was three times in one day.

I was surrounded by rivers that threatened to rise above my head and had flame-filled trails to walk. But God promised they wouldn't overtake me and made sure I knew He was right there with me. I was told over and over terrible things were coming with this round of chemo, but I rejected the fear and held onto God's promises. I knew He was in control, so I had to keep my mind in that place. He was and is the Ultimate Healer.

Though the kitchen-sink treatment was indeed wicked, I endured with flying colors. In fact, I suffered no adverse side effects at all—a true miracle. The doctors were continually stunned, and some of them even said, "You don't even need us!" My simple reply was, "That's how my God works."

Early on, we knew I would need a stem cell transplant. Aside from that complicated procedure, there was a lot that had to happen: I had to get in remission, find a good donor match, ward off infections, do the transplant, and then survive 100 days before I could return home. The delay in remission and additional rounds of chemo—along with other surprise hospitalizations—kept throwing off my calendar. And I wanted to get home. My prayer angel, Renee Ingle, told me a truth that evaporated all of my fear and frustration, "God is going to have the right donor at the right time." I stood on those words, proclaimed them repeatedly, and kept doing everything I could to keep my mind and body healthy. Keeping my lungs in great shape was especially important to combat pneumonia. So I actually danced through the halls every day and listened to music. I chose to dance in this place that saw so much despair because I was dancing with my God in the face of death.

During the wait, I rented an apartment within a few minutes of the hospital. Even with the apartment I still spent ten-plus hours per day multiple days of the week at the hospital. I came first thing in the morning, going from appointment to appointment, walking and resting whenever I could. However, I'll never forget what spending so much time on the MDA campus was like.

LIFE AT MDA

When arriving at MD Anderson, it was like walking into a sea of sickness. Everywhere were bald people, wearing masks and gloves, drenched in dread and exhaustion. And who could blame them? They had been plucked from their lives just like I was from mine.

Consider that many leukemia patients had labs every Monday, Wednesday, and Friday, and were in need of blood or platelets. Monday labs were especially busy because of the weekend, leaving 24 hours in which patients weren't checked. Then, if someone's counts were low or their body was unable to produce red blood cells or platelets, it was time for a transfusion.

I soon learned that most everybody was tense on Mondays, so I started to bring little bags of candy that each had a positive quote on one side and "Happy Monday" written on the other. I also added a label that read, "Attitude is everything" with a picture of Mt. Rushmore and the words, "South Dakota rocks, thanks for all you do, Carolyn Thompson." I always tried to create light in a situation where it seemed the lights were going out for many people. Soon after, the lights turned on for me.

THE TRANSPLANT

Four months to the day after I started my hospitalization, I received my stem cell transplant. It was a success, and I began my hundred-day journey toward home. The post-stem cell life was even more grueling than the pre-stem cell. We were always on guard for viral, fungal, or bacterial risks, along with cell rejection, and I received a barrage of medication that practically needed a pharmacy degree to administer. Typically, I had three meds that changed two to three times per week, in addition to the twelve others I took four different times per day. I took some twelve hours apart, some with food, some on an empty stomach, and still others had contingencies like, "Make sure not to take this one within two hours of that one." I became a pro at flushing my lines (whether it be a PICC in my arm or lumens in my chest), and adhered to their warnings: no exposure to the sun, rain, wind, or large crowds; and no ingestion of raw fruits or vegetables. It really was a full-time job being an AML patient, but I needed my life to consist of more than just being a patient.

As part of my treatment, I had daily infusions at the infusion center. These were always tense situations for the nurses. A lot of the patients were perpetually frustrated because of frequent delays—often hours long—to get their room. So many variables were at play that delays became inevitable. Patients were late; appointments got backed up; someone's line clotted up and needed to be de-clotted, and the list went on. I could see the stress written across the brow of every nurse. So I took it upon myself to talk to and encourage them.

I revisited my entrepreneurial roots and looked at how I could make a bigger impact with the amount of time I spent there. After some scheming, my Thompson Law team helped me create postcards with the outline of South Dakota and a star marking Sioux Falls, and I took these and wrote positive messages to different nurses, using key phrases or Scripture based on a particular point that we were trying to resolve in his or her life. It could have been a desire for more effective communication with patients, issues with their family, or any other rub in their life that they wanted to resolve. They just needed some encouragement, and I was there to do it and wanted to leave them with something tangible. I appreciated the great care they provided me.

I was also very intentional about using the nurses' names. It was hard because there were so many of them, but they were important to me, and I wanted them to know that. I wanted to honor the golden rule and treat others how I wanted to be treated. I was a person, not a patient, and I would cling to that no matter what the diagnosis or challenge of the day was. I learned that sometimes people are in our storm to help; other times, we're in theirs to do the same.

MY PEOPLE

The most difficult part of my journey, though, was being away from my children. I desperately wanted to be there for them through each of their major life events and to help them weather every storm. I had done my own legacy and estate planning, so I knew my family was secure. Even though I had confidence my kids would be okay, the most difficult thought to bear was missing their lives. Life is about who we're with, and I wanted to be with them.

Back home, I also knew my Thompson Law family and my clients were secure. All of my succession plans were ironclad; insurance was covered, and we had a written Emergency Operations Plan in place—which I will share more about in chapter seven. Just like the building, we'd constructed the firm so it was built to last.

Some people found the Lord when they were afraid. I always knew He was present, but how I grew most was when His peace came over me. I experienced firsthand that I was with Him, and He was with me. If the Lord said, "Carolyn, you're coming home," then I was going home. I knew He had a great and mighty purpose, and I wasn't going through this battle alone. The next level in my growth was seeking His peace and learning to wait well. I'm sure Jesus did not enjoy the brutality He endured, but He trusted the Father—and if He did, I would too.

Though it saddened me to imagine missing my kids' lives, I knew their future was secure, and I knew my Thompson Law team would be safe as well. We'd worked diligently to prepare well for the unexpected. So as I healed and battled for remission, I was able to rest in the Lord and the understanding that He'd already prepared a way for all of us. We were in the palm of His hand, and there was nowhere safer to be.

In total, I spent eight months away from home, but all the while I lived the reality of God's promise from Philippians 4:6-7:

Do not be anxious about anything, but in everything by prayer and supplication with thanksgiving let your requests be made known to God. And the peace of God, which surpasses all understanding, will guard your hearts and your minds in Christ Jesus.

5 FOLLOWING THE LEADER

God allows trials to shape and change us—most importantly, though, to increase our faith. Learning to fully depend on Him through everything—from the building project to my cancer journey—had rippled into everything. The firm has had this quality especially woven into it.

As an entrepreneur, I'd learned my first and most important job was to listen and move with the Lord. When I followed His lead, everything fell into place; our team was in sync; our clients were well cared for, and my kids got exactly what they needed. Fortunately, these truths had been with us from the very beginning.

FAITH, FAMILY, FIRM

When I was called to create Thompson Law on my own, I recall thinking I could do it. I could do the math, interpret analytics, and set all the right metrics to make a successful business. But what mattered most was that I'd followed the Lord and made an environment conducive for growth. In this, I experienced an incredible freedom—I call it a *scary fantastic freedom*—when I completely trusted God. Instead of it being up to me, it was up to Him, and I was simply to follow. Do you know how freeing that is?

This was where my decision-making paradigm came from: faith, family, firm. Faced with any given scenario, these are the questions I ask and how I prioritize the answers. First, I ask what my faith is telling me. Is God calling me to zig when common wisdom says zag? Second, how healthy are my team member's families, the families we serve, and my own family? Third and finally, how will our footprint be affected? Is it a good move to grow the firm, or will it make us vulnerable in the long term?

BEING A LEADER WHO IS LED

As an entrepreneur, I've learned to be dependent on God in all circumstances. Facing projects like our building or my journey through cancer are obvious milestones. But I've learned to trust Him in subtler ways, too. Even when it seems small, God shows up. I'd been at points of sheer exhaustion, and my tank had run dry, but there were still appointments left in the day. In these times, I've prayed, "Holy Spirit, I need you. I need you. I need you. We're serving families today." And the energy comes.

See, it takes intense listening to help the families I work with. There is so much more at play than numbers on a spreadsheet.

There are years of family dynamics, past wounds, and future hopes all wrapped up in our work. So I don't have a job where I can simply show up to the office and check out. When I'm with people, I'm really *with* them; it's my calling. When I've needed energy and endurance, the Lord has supplied. And what's always incredible is that even on days when I shouldn't be standing, He infuses me with such clarity, focus, and ability to connect, it only points back to Him.

Leaning on God in the big things can be scary, but I've learned that depending on Him through everything—even the small stuff—is truly a joy. Faith can run through our entire life, from morning to evening, from appointment to appointment, and office to office. And everything we do takes on deeper meaning and value, not just for us, but for those we serve as well.

In retrospect, building our building was just like constructing a church. It turned into a space where people are helped and healed, where they find security and wounds are mended. Thompson Law has become a place where I minister as much as work. This is the vision and promise of our priorities: *faith, family, firm.*

In sum, these three words mean that a will is not just a will. A trust is not just a trust. These are people's lives. How our clients' final chapters are written is completely dependent upon how their legacy plan is crafted. People work so hard for their entire lives, so I believe my calling is to work hard alongside them and protect what they've worked for—and beyond the assets, the family itself. But to run a firm that keeps that at the forefront takes faith that honoring people honors God. However, as a leader, I am tasked with the responsibility to lead while following Him.

THE BALANCING ACT

To do this means finding the right balance in life and business. As an entrepreneur, I know anything measurable can be improved. I've learned this through creating efficient business systems and looking for constant improvements. There's also a place where I'm humbled before the Lord, seeking His will: spending daily time in prayer, petition, and studying His word. These two facets of my life meet each time I make a decision. However, one doesn't dominate the other.

I certainly wouldn't have a firm, a building, and a healthy body if I'd simply hoped God would do everything for me. I certainly listened intently and trusted Him, but I also had to measure and execute the right decisions. This is the balance of Christian entrepreneurship. We need the right people at the right time to do the right thing. So I pray for the right clients, make every effort to hire the right people, and then ensure we're doing the right things as they present themselves. And sometimes, it looks different than expected.

When a great opportunity presents itself, we're often quick to say yes. However, I've learned that we need to pray about everything— even the good things. A while back, the Lutheran Synod representatives approached me to lead a Givers for Life project. I had previously led some local sessions, and they thought a video of me would allow their churches across the country to have a consistent message on giving and estate planning.

At first sight, this was something I wanted to jump on. It was in line with our values and would be an excellent partnership for both myself and Thompson Law. However, I prayed about it, and to my surprise, the Lord told me no. It was a surprise, but I heard Him clearly. So I thanked them for this very flattering offer and declined. Times like these may be some of the most difficult for us to trust Him. There are few things harder in business than saying no to a great offer on the table.

Six weeks went by from when I declined, and I continued to pray. Then, one morning, He told me it was time to do it! He laid Genesis 22 on my heart, and I understood what He was teaching me.

In Genesis 22, we find Abraham taking his only son Isaac to a mountain. But God told Abraham to do something unthinkable. He was to sacrifice his son Isaac, even though this was the boy God had promised to him years earlier. Abraham was bewildered and confused, but he obeyed. Then on top of that mountain, just as the knife was about to fall, an angel intervened and provided a different route. God had never intended for Abraham to sacrifice his son, but He did intend to keep Abraham's heart completely dependent upon Himself.

As a leader, I'm constantly checking in with the Lord and have come to trust Him even when it's confusing or contrary to all business sense. However, when I'm doing my part as a diligent business owner *and* listening to God's voice, everything seems to sing—eventually. His plans are always right, even if not on our schedule or in our comfort zone. The best part is that not only are we fulfilled, but this is where our clients are best served as well. *Scary fantastic freedom, it is a great place to be.*

This requires I also be ready for God's next curveball, too, though. Because every time He does the unexpected, He's giving me a chance to grow. Before I got sick, I actually had the thought that, "Uh-oh, things are getting too easy. It's time to grow again." Little did I know the path I would walk. But grow I did, and not just me, but everyone on my team as well.

When I filter my business analysis through God's Word, I feel very connected to God and to people. I sense His protection and know He's already gone ahead of me. He knows what's around every corner and understands what every person who walks into our office needs. Our team is just as important as our clients.

Sometimes the measure of a business's success is based on revenues or number of clients, but I wanted to create a place where team members could grow personally and professionally. I wanted our employees to look back and say their lives were better for the time they spent at Thompson Law. I have learned that people come into our life "for a reason, a season, or a lifetime," and it's best to appreciate the positive aspects of the time together. As a close mentor once reminded me, Jesus's first focus was on His disciples. So I have a picture of the Last Supper that reminds me that it's not just okay, but it's right, to focus on my team.

THE HARVEST WILL COME

Much like the farmers I work with, my duty is to invest in the right places. Each year, I have to plant my seed at the right time then tend it in the right way, all the while trusting that a harvest is going to come in its time. For me, the harvest can be income, but it can also be people, deepened connections, and relationships.

At any point in my journey, if I had neglected God's leading and said no to planting those seeds, I would look back in regret. I would feel as if I had denied the greatest voice of all because I'd clung to my earthly security. It would mean all of the families we've helped and the stories we've been a part of would be gone. We wouldn't have had a hand in their lives, and neither would they in ours. Following Him, no matter how hard, has always been the best decision.

Through it all, my experiences personally and at Thompson Law have continually led me deeper with the Lord. They've always propelled me along a path of trust and peace. I believe that I only serve a loving God, and He will only ask me to take the path that benefits me or someone else the most. This belief is really at the core of my faith and my experiences.

My God is loving, which means all I will experience from Him is love. I may not always understand it at the time, but I trust Him beyond my circumstances. Looking back at everything I've been through, I see God's shadow right beside me. I know that if I can make it as far as I've come, I can make it through anything, and not because of my strength or ability, but because of how faithful He is. My job is to listen and obey, because when God moves, I have to move with Him or face the regret of missing out.

PART THREE

CONNECTION

6 DEEP ROOTS

I love trees and have many on my property, and I am so thankful for the people who planted them before me. Much of my life and estate-planning practice is spent thinking about a different kind of tree, though: the family tree. We live, from one generation to the next, connected to each other. Just like the trees on my property, our shared context, beauty, and challenge make us who we are. Our roots grow together. Which means the deeper our roots, the better we can serve those around us.

GOING DEEP IN DRY TIMES

Did you know that trees extend their roots deeper in times of drought? The hotter and drier it is on top of the soil, the further down they need to dig. They search out the water, curling around every rock in their way. These trees that withstand drought are the ones that can also weather the storms. Their roots become so deep and extensive that they aren't toppled by the wind. They're too firmly planted in the soil to be uprooted. The drought has made them heartier, tougher, and a deeper part of the landscape.

We're not so different from the trees. My life in the hospital was filled with the continual drought of bad news, threatening to turn my internal landscape into dust. I was bombarded with constant difficulty and disappointment, but I rejected it. And as I did, people watered, nourished, and cared for me. My roots grew deeper through that difficult season. As I've reached out and people have learned my story, I've had just as many respond that they're growing in their faith through my journey.

See, the deeper our roots extend, the broader our reach, the further our branches unfurl, and the more shade we can cast. We also bear fruit that can nourish others by standing on God's promises no matter the circumstances. Our attitude must be, *We are going to go through it, but are we growing through it?*

NO PATH OF ROSES

In life, being a Christian certainly doesn't mean getting to walk a path of roses. Human lives were never promised to be trouble free; in fact, the opposite is true. Jesus Himself walked the *Via Dolorosa*, Latin for the "Way of Grief." It still exists to this day and is a winding street through the Old City of Jerusalem that is said to be the path Jesus walked on His way to the cross. The apostles faced more than their fair share of hardships as well.

We cannot control what happens to us, but we can control our response to it. We can either allow ourselves to fall into a pity party, saying, "Poor me," to everyone we meet. Or we can say, "I'm going to make it through this." The key to this mindset is advanced decision making. We simply don't give ourselves a choice. There's not an option on the table where we don't make it through our trials and hardships. Instead, our default mode becomes *persevere.*

This produces tenacity in our lives and a resolve to do the right thing at the right time for the right reasons—even if it's hard to do so. Often, the hardest thing to do will be to follow the Lord through difficult times. I want to leave this Earth knowing that I did follow Him, that I did what He asked no matter the cost, and that I rejected fear and accepted His strength in faith.

WHEN FOLLOWING GOD DOESN'T FEEL GOOD

Understand that God is always going to call us to the harder thing. This is especially tough when family or friends begin saying, "You are crazy for doing this. . . ." But when the Lord calls us to move, we move with Him. Through my cancer journey, I've come to view seasons of pain, fear, and discomfort through a different lens. Through this I also learned a lot about acceptance: accepting I had to do what I had to do and accepting that life would be different now, but most of all, learning to find joy in the journey no matter what came at me, because He was with me, always.

I've learned to wait well. I know that He is always at work, and I trust He is with me. So even when things seem to have slowed to a crawl when I want to run, I wait. I trust. I watch and listen for His time, because it's always perfect. I've realized growing in our faith can mean letting God into every aspect of our lives. And this can be seen so much clearer when we wait on Him, trusting in Him for all things.

After having heard countless painful stories from my clients, I had resolved that, even before my cancer, we only serve a loving God. I don't always get to understand the why, so instead I choose to trust. There is always a reason for the storm. Sometimes stuff has to wash away, or blighted branches need to be pruned. But whether we're in the sunshine or a dark pit, turn to Paul: "Rejoice in the Lord always; again I will say, rejoice" (Philippians 4:4). The goal of my life has become contentment, which to me, means living amid a deep understanding that God is with me, and I am with Him. Every moment of every day, I can rejoice because He is near.

Even while undergoing intense chemo that felt like I was spitting out fire, I knew I was going to get through it. I wouldn't accept any other truth. I prayed, "Father, thank You for choosing me to be the mom to Taylor, Rachel and Will, and I am the mother I need to be. Thank You that I'm well able to serve the families that You send. Thank You that I am healed." I'm content because I'm praying with confidence coupled with an attitude that says, "Nevertheless, Your will, and not mine, be done." Because God's will is always good. His signature move is to make good out of bad circumstances. They say we can't come out gold unless we go through the fire.

THE RIGHT PEOPLE

Throughout my journey, God has also sent the right people right when I needed them. When I first underwent treatment in Texas, it became clear I was going to need to hire someone to help me with certain aspects of my life, things like cleaning, cooking, and all sorts of things that I never thought I would need help with. I was very fortunate I had had a long-term-care insurance policy as a young, healthy adult. After having seen so many clients go through horrific situations, I knew I needed to cover this risk.

It took awhile for me to find the right fit, as these were very specialized, personal services. At times, I needed someone, while at other times I was doing better and could manage on my own. So it was a winding path to find the right person. Then I met Alexis.

Alexis, I would later learn, was from the Congo. He was tall, thin, quiet, but most of all a wonderful man. On his first day he asked me if I was a Christian, and I replied yes. After we spoke more he said he'd suspected as much after seeing the kind of books I read and the way I acted. We connected instantly, and he was a gift from God—but for more than I expected. The coming season would be very difficult for me. I was on several high doses of medication and suffered from an intense lack of sleep, so I needed Alexis to be there more often. Once, I remember asking him if he would have dinner with me and if we could pray.

I'd shared different parts of my journey and how God had always been four steps ahead of me and had prepared the way for my cancer journey.

He said, "Ms. Carolyn, you didn't know it, but when I first met you, I was in your bathroom on my knees, and I prayed to the Lord for your journey. Not your health, but your journey."

Alexis then shared he had three prayer partners at his church, and they had all been praying for my journey since he began helping me. Now, most people who see a cancer patient over 1,000 miles from her home and family would pray for her health. But he innately knew it was a journey of faith for me, not cancer. God placed him in my life at the perfect moment so that I could grow. See, he, too, had been on an amazing walk with the Lord. His trials and faith served to help me through mine.

At my inquiry, he explained to me how his government in the Congo legalized it for a certain class, the Hutus, to kill any of his class, the Tutsis, and that many of his family members had been killed. His government announced on the radio that it was legal to kill anyone in the Tutsi class; the government even provided weapons. He had wounds on his legs where he'd been shot, and despite all of this terror, he still knew and trusted the Lord. He had an amazing heart of forgiveness and trust, and God could not have placed a better, more trusting caregiver to help me grow.

After a life of helping people and being helped myself, I've realized we're all fundamentally the same. We just come in different packages. We each need the same things, and God sends us the right people exactly when we need them. They become part of how our roots are deepened, and in turn, we are used by God to help others grow, too.

7 WHO WE'RE WITH

People and relationships are the most important things in life, both the ones we need and the ones who need us. In our culture, though, this is easy to get confused. We often focus on records, accomplishments, and bottom lines over the people themselves. What truly matters isn't what we achieve, but who we're with.

One evening, when my son Taylor was just a baby, I held him in a wooden rocking chair. He was precious and perfect, cuddled up to me in his little sleeper. A baseball game played on TV, and a famous player had just hit a record-breaking home run. It seemed like the world erupted for a moment, and everyone thought it was so amazing. What I remember, though, was looking at him and realizing it didn't matter what records I achieved. Life was about who I was with, and I wanted him to know and live that, too. I wanted to be with this child into eternity, and that was why being rooted and grounded in the Lord was what mattered most.

From the start, I've held people as the core priority at our firm, and this started with the team members themselves. Every time I interviewed a new candidate, I would ask myself two questions. First, "Would I sit on a boat alone with this person for two hours?" And second, "Would I trust this person with my children?" These are such important questions because they cut right to the heart of what's most important: the people we surround ourselves with. I couldn't imagine working with people who didn't meet those two standards. Not only do I like and trust the people on my team, but I also want to take care of them in tangible ways. While it's nice to tell people how much we appreciate them, it's vital to make sure the ones who count on us are secure.

PROTECTING WHAT MATTERS MOST

In the decade leading up to my radical sabbatical, I'd crafted an emergency plan that would take effect should something ever happen to me. I'm so grateful I took the time to do this when I did, as it paid dividends in protecting my family, my team, and my clients. Because my biggest values are people and relationships, I couldn't leave their care open-ended if I could do something to prevent disaster for them. Our entire practice is dedicated to estate planning and business succession. Our goal is to make sure a family stays a family, a business stays a business (Thompson Law included), and a farm stays a farm.

I'd like to share with you the emergency plan I crafted as a testimony to God's preparation for both my family and my firm. You can have insight into how you can plan to care for your business, family, and legacy in advance. We protect what matters most to us, and this was a way I worked to do that—and I'm so grateful I did.

CRAFTING A PLAN

Each year, I had a standing appointment on April 15th to read, review, and revise a written Emergency Operations Plan. (And as God's timing would have it, I bumped this decision up early the year I underwent cancer treatment because of our Reflect and Connect event.) I would assess and make sure it adequately met our needs, sign it, and then share the updated version with the five-person management team I'd assigned. Should I be out of the picture for any reason, I had a team that would swoop in and work the plan, consisting of a communications director, an operations manager, a trusted external CPA, and two attorneys of their choosing.

Communications Director

Some think if the leader dies, so does the business, because both the employees and clients will scatter. So my first priority, should something ever happen to me, was communicating the internal state of Thompson Law, and this fell to the communications director. This leader had full authority over what details would be shared, when, and with whom. I also made sure this person understood this idea thoroughly: "There is no such thing as over-communication!"

If something tragic happens, a company cannot afford to lose control of communication and perception in the marketplace. My top concern was to make sure everyone knew that just because something happened to me, Thompson Law was here to stay, steel footings and all. I also knew to ensure my employees understood their jobs were secure, insurance was paid, and there was space to breathe. This was the core of the communications director's job, and it was exceptionally important.

Operations Manager

Next, I'd select an emergency operations manager every year. This person's role was to oversee the day-to-day work, ensuring teams were cared for and new clients were onboarded well. We have systems for how we care for clients, but if we didn't have someone in place to maintain them, how would they be further developed, expanded, and implemented?

In turn, this would also provide the internal team a sense of stability because even though something major has happened, the company continues to follow our standard operating procedures. Those procedures and systems are so important that we invested considerable time and dollars developing them. So they needed someone to continue driving them forward.

CPA

If we remove the primary producer from a business, we need to have another way to keep cash flow in place. That may seem like an obvious statement, but if I hadn't planned for that contingency before the unexpected happened, my team would have been scrambling and in reactionary mode. This is why the third person I invited into my emergency team was an external CPA whom I trusted and worked closely with. I wanted someone who knew the key indicators of our cash flow and timing and could be the financial eyes on the ground. There are no words that can express my gratitude for all Mary Dally has done for me. She is far, far more than an excellent CPA and advisor. It is crucial that we have someone in our court who sees us as more than just another client.

In all, I picked these people because they knew my business philosophy and understood I led from a connected heart and head. And each year, when I reviewed the plan and the list of names, I'd also ensure we had other guardrails in place as well. I created sample press releases and client letters for every event from if I were to become disabled to my untimely death. We had overhead insurance and enough financial reserves to weather the extremely unlikely scenario that the firm brought in no revenue for several months.

If anything were to ever happen, this team and this plan would become the functional leader of Thompson Law. So when *something big did happen*, I praised God I'd taken the time to prepare. And not only was it good for my people, it was healing for me.

The stress of cancer is so intense, this peace of mind propelled my healing exponentially. This alleviated the fear my business would crumble because each year, I clearly saw the plan for how it would succeed without me. Having worked shoulder to shoulder, brain to brain, and heart to heart for so many years with the Thompson Law team, I knew I could trust them with it all.

When we focus on who we're with and how to care for them over achievements, records, revenue—*or anything else*—we find peace and fulfillment beyond words. As I've shared, I've been through some difficult, even death-defying, times. However, what I consistently found true was that I only serve a loving God, and He has provided for both myself and the people I love most. I believe if we put our faith in this, we will find it to prove just as true and experience the same peace I have been blessed with every day of my life.

CONCLUSION

My working life began in a small town, in my family's business, and alongside farmers and their families. Those are my people and are still whom I work with and serve to this day. When we focus on people, then we can find and fulfill our purpose.

I've dedicated my life to keeping a family a family, a farm a farm, and a business a business. I've done so at Thompson Law but in my own life as well. Caring for my children has taught me about God's love and providence as much as anything, if not more.

In writing this book and reflecting on my journey from the Corner Cafe to a business of my own to the unexpected twist of MD Anderson, I'm reminded of God's hand at work through it all. It is not lost on me that I was blessed with a blood cancer. Just as the donor's cells gave me new life, my new life only comes from Christ, His blood, His sacrifice, and His love. Mostly, He has provided for me through the right people at the right time so I could make the right decisions. The guidance from a spiritual mentor to build our building showed me when He's moving, I need to follow. The encouragement from my friends, family, and even strangers through my cancer journey allowed me to hear God's voice exactly when I needed it.

Looking at my son Taylor in the rocking chair taught me who we're with is the greatest gift of all. I could write another book full of more God stories, more times when He came through when I needed Him.

I'm grateful for the people He's placed in my life, and I anticipate what lies ahead. My vision will remain the same because it's where I find peace and fulfillment. I only serve a loving God who lives in a place four steps ahead of us all. Everything He does, gives us, and challenges us with is because of His love. I get to live in that *scary fantastic freedom* that can only come from Him. I don't say this from naiveté, either. I say this from living through a life brimming with promises kept and life secured. I live to help people preserve the families and legacies God has gifted to them, because I have learned there is simply nothing more precious. In honoring you and your story, we honor Him.

ACKNOWLEDGEMENTS

Many times, I have gone through my life and caught myself saying, "There is nothing I have done well enough to deserve this person in my life." There are so many of these people who have profoundly impacted my life in ways that they may never know. This began long before my cancer journey. Our closeness did not need cancer to be the connection. Whether a client, a colleague or a friend, I hold a special place in my heart for you. What I love about life is that love can take on so many forms, and the more we love, the more we can love—our heart just expands. Thankfully we lived a life free from guardrails so that we could connect and say what needed to be said. Thank you for helping me grow in so many ways. There are so many people whom I love and felt loved by. I can't mention everyone here, but I hope you all know how truly thankful I am that you have been a part of my life.

With that, I am going to mention some who were instrumental in my life and in my journey thus far.

The work that I did at New Haven Ministries in Sioux Falls, South Dakota, took me on a completely different trajectory with my walk with the Lord. Certainly, I knew Jesus as my Lord and Savior and had surrendered my life well before I was introduced to New Haven, but their biblical life coaching has brought me into a relationship with the Lord that I never knew could exist, and I am still growing to this day. Clearly, they're one of my top nonprofit organizations.

At Thompson Law, there were some who not only took on additional business obligations, but cared for me as a person, not just their employer. Special thanks to Elise Knobloch, Sandra Hensch and Rebecca Longcrow. Of course, we could not have survived without our long-term team members Renee Mettler and Elaine Rye. During my creative days Elizabeth Burns was on her game, to help me in completing many of my joy-on-the-journey projects. The American Academy of Estate Planning Attorneys, its founders and members are vital to our success, and I feel many of them are some of my best friends in the world.

Love knows no bounds. I want to thank the many people who reached out to me and kept my spirits high—whether cheering me on from afar or near. Your prayers, well wishes, cards, texts, emails and gift packages were appreciated so much. I would like to mention a special thank you to everyone but that listing might be longer than the book! Receiving the hundreds and hundreds of cards made me feel so connected (special thanks to Penny Paclik and Jim Woster who didn't let a week go by without my receiving a card in the mail and to Julie Iverson's daily email that included words of God's faithfulness). The following people deserve special recognition for visiting me while I was receiving medical care at the MD Anderson Cancer Center in Houston, Texas: My SD crew, including Mike Luken, Rachel Thompson, Will Thompson, Taylor Thompson, Sandy Hensch, Elise Knobloch, Pastor Lance Rensch, Cheryl

Stevens, Tammy Ludeman, Mary Howard, Bruce & Carrie Wintle, Heather Springer, Donna Roti, Stacy Mongar, Mary Ann Gengler, Zach Fontenille; and Deb Sexton (AK), Dan & Kathy Morris (AZ), Jennifer Price (CA), Catherine Hammond (CO), Lucy Lui (China), Kevin Merrigan (FL), Adrianna Fontenille (MN), Tom Paige (MN), Art Stevens (NC), Kat Beaulieu & Silvein (Quebec), Heidi Weelborg (TX), and Doug Traylor (TX).

As God would have it, there were many people I met in Texas who are now woven into my life forever: Melissa Deaton, Becky Parker, Sara Trainor, Seaumus Nasser, Donna Swain, Alexis, LuLu Rodriquez, and AC Conrad.

ABOUT THE AUTHOR

Carolyn A. Thompson

Carolyn A. Thompson founded Thompson Law, P.C. in 2003 to create an estate- and business-planning law firm that helps pass on the legacy, values, and stewardship of its clients. Carolyn has sought out, developed, and trained attorneys dedicated to listening to a client's life story, including their goals and concerns, and to creating a customized estate or business plan to address the individual circumstances of each client. Carolyn describes herself as an entrepreneur with the heart of a teacher who happens to practice law in the beautiful world of keeping families families, farms farms, and businesses businesses. The goal of the Thompson Law, P.C. team is to positively impact families for generations to come.

Outside of the firm, Carolyn enjoys traveling and spending time with her three amazing children, Taylor, Rachel and Will.

ABOUT THOMPSON LAW

Thompson Law, P.C. is an estate- and business-planning law firm dedicated to providing its clients with quality estate-planning resources.

The mission statement of the Thompson Law team is to help people leave a legacy for their loved ones, not solely in terms of financial means, but also with a reflection of the values and the beliefs that can be shared with generations to come.

Located in Sioux Falls, Thompson Law, P.C. holds the sole membership for South Dakota (and parts of Iowa and Minnesota) in the American Academy of Estate Planning Attorneys, a national organization focused on serving the needs of estate-planning attorneys and helping them deliver the highest possible service to their clients. The Academy is an exclusive organization whose members must complete ongoing, extensive education requirements in advanced business and estate planning.

Team members at Thompson Law, P.C. are licensed to serve clients in South Dakota, North Dakota, Minnesota, and Iowa.

More information about Carolyn and Thompson Law, P.C. is available online at www.cathompsonlaw.com.

Made in the USA
Lexington, KY
17 April 2017